Touched

Luther Hughes

Sibling Rivalry Press
Little Rock, Arkansas
DISTURB/ENRAPTURE

Touched
Copyright © 2018 by Luther Hughes

Cover art, *Embracing*, by Jalen Miller
Cover design by Seth Pennington and Bryan Borland
Cover design by Kathryn Leland
Author photograph by Robert Strong

All rights reserved. No part of this book may be reproduced or republished without written consent from the publisher, except by reviewers who may quote brief excerpts in connection with a review in a newspaper, magazine, or electronic publication; nor may any part of this book be reproduced, stored in a retrieval system, or transmitted in any form, or by any means be recorded without written consent of the publisher.

Sibling Rivalry Press, LLC
PO Box 26147
Little Rock, AR 72221

info@siblingrivalrypress.com

www.siblingrivalrypress.com

ISBN: 978-1-943977-45-1

This title is housed permanently in the Rare Books and Special Collections Vault of the Library of Congress.

First Sibling Rivalry Press Edition, January 2018

for my mother

CONTENTS

Touched

Why you wanna fly Blackbird you ain't ever gonna fly

- Nina Simone, "Blackbird"

Hominal

There's abuse.
The hands of the thing.

The nailed digits. Everything an aperture.
A dead animal.

Licking. Grazing.
The couch-skirt against concrete.

Where the walls mate.
The bathroom door lilts.

A loose tooth in a child's gum.

I watch my reflection in the sliding door.
A dead animal.
I watch myself crane.
Throat clutching sounds.

Everything is allowed
to prey.

See the fist. Like shale.
Meeting my spine.
Meaning slay.

Stretch me. Relax.
Something about skinned alive.

When to bleed. When to bleed.

Something family
to human. Not the bone.
But the bone

broken
through.

What's left of sounds tease the graveyard.

Everything is flight.
The eyes relinquish light.
Peel to darkness.

Who prepared me?

In the beginning.
I was dirt. Am dirt.

Then molecule. Then fluid. Then sinew.

—I watched the body
grow humongous

then sing a little boy

How We Forget

I forgot I had skin   forgot what happens

to bones   when they are swamped   in sin

bed sheets   I forgot about the bed sheets

forgot the nights he buried my name

            with his fists   forgot I had fists too

forgot I had lips to scream   I have forgotten how

        to scream   forgotten how to pray

didn't forget I was his prey   forgot to feel

        ashamed   forgot what I looked like

in the mirror   forgot that my eyes matched my skin

if only I remembered my skin I forgot to blink

        to breathe in between the minutes

forgot I had lungs to inhale   forgot how to inhale

didn't forget I had holes   didn't forget humans

are made of holes   forgot we all end up in

     holes   did I mention my skin   still no

memory of what skin looks like wrapped in soil

forgot skin soils   I forgot myself

and the language of sorry   and stop   and no

     and don't   and please

forgot where I go   when I die

     is it heaven   or my backyard

forgot that black fades after awhile

     forgot humans fade too

sometimes we are left to wear the words

of others to   keep from committing suicide

I forgot how to commit suicide   is it before

     or after the bed sheets

should I wait before or after the end

And the Lord said unto Cain, Where *is* Abel thy brother? And
he said, I know not: *Am* I my brother's keeper?

-Genesis 4:9

Offering

I.

At the end of the day, agony
is a mouth. In the mirror, I watch
the mouth shiver. If it's not
the warmth of knowing, then it's nothing.
Here me: I was taken
to the basement. There was a couch
I slid between. Then darkness.
Outside of me, my brother
marveled at my inner workings.
The porous moon stumbled into
the sliding doors. Covered.
He plunged until couldn't, stiff sounds
of flesh smacking flesh. I imagined
how blood responded to intrusion.
The static dance. And then
I didn't. Ache became
the bones' framework. We severed
the house. The city. I ruined
commands: *Stop. Ouch.* My brother
was hypnotized, powerless
to curiosity. As night cleaved, so did he,
catching a new wind, watching skin halve.
Who to slur? I don't know.
But lovers have asked
about bruises left when it was over.
The couch still a couch. The basement learned
me. I'm still taken. I have a mirror.

II.

When the snake sewn to your hips hummed
a head of glass inside me, I refused. The reptile
begged to braid the vessel, become breath
before the blood spread.

Relax, you said. Breathe.
I relaxed. Counted the clock with a hymn:

> *no weapons*
> *formed against me*
> *shall prosper*

You flowered the room with my lungs, flung
me into the couch, to the walls, against
the fireplace. "I own you."
You made me hear it—*own*—
with the knuckles' belted cry.
It roiled from your lips
as panic spilled moths from—forget it.

This was your love: if not the body,
then the blood. If not the blood, pray
alone in the cold basement

—let me start over. When finished
I absorbed the remains. Held between
organs.   You left not telling
tomorrow or how to mend the brown skin once torn.

Bird with Two Backs

Now your briefs. I felt him still into a wing,
sweep. The blinds carved moonlight onto
the bed sheets. The mirror, hung beside the
doorway, winked. I fanned my naked into
the moon's milked eye. My hands curled a
dead dahlia. He would dance the dance of the
peacock. Shimmer a mural until mounting.

Clenched

around the thyroid, your palm is
a wide-stitch grin. I—splayed
open to pieces, made slaughterhouse red.

I wasn't sorry. The next day, I wanted
you. I—splayed to pieces, made slaughterhouse.

When you reached the bladder,
there was God. Like you, he was
insistent. Would vein the spine.
Would you believe all my insides
kept: wires, tendons, fluids.

I wasn't grateful. I was bloodlust
revisited. I—pieces, slaughterhouse . . .
Revisited.
            I. I. I.

Tenderness

When the festival was over, I watched the crows
pluck the earth until sour. I wavered, nestled
the scene inside the contour of my eyes. I wasn't
a violent person. Had I'd been. Had my feet desired the reverb
of the fowl's hollow,
I would have fled. Instead, I write
my brother's forced sex.
"Relax" in italics. Being a beast
of craft, I grew ill. Gave my earth to a man
with no parade in his body. It didn't matter.
The man clipped my pelvis at the smile, searched
for the muscle. A familiar rummaging.
Outside his bedroom window, perched
atop a pine tree, my brother
watched: the gelled underpink
exposed, the swift choke flattening
the neck, the flourishing of him, him, him.
How wild to watch an animal die.
Do nothing. When I speak of cruelty, I mean
"do nothing." I confess: I craved my brother gutted. Let me
take the crow's toothed
black, bury it.

A Question of Rain

Admit it,
being wet is the only option. You
crawl outside, throw yourself against the
drain—it's better this way. Pushing your
ethereal against the metal ribs of the curb's
     curl and
finish.
     All you have is your moist. Your
gout-lip when
he slips, sinks beneath your skin. What terrifies
isn't the storm, but the looming light afterwards.
     The pearled sky silent as a seed.
Just as rain, you were born to be there.
     And then not. Like
kinfolk.
Luther, you thought you could walk on water. His
mouth sly, slick against your corpse.
Now, he says.
Open.   This is what happens when two things
     meet. The flesh turns inward like a fist,
       starved and thirsty. The earth
pining for a boy
quieted.   You don't know the meaning
     of emptiness. It can't be
removed. It
succumbs to the single
tongue's whip.
Under all that mess is more mess,
venerating the wash of what you can handle.
     You.
wail
exactly how you envisioned.
You hear it? You hear
Zion?

Any Black Thing

Because it's the same basement
the story doesn't change. He comes
with fists—knuckles cut into copper
bullets—readied for what's to come.
I don't notice the variance
in voice. The way he tails between words.
But who's counting. When he lights
the fireplace, he uses a match found
beneath the couch, strikes it once, throws it
into the hearth. He wants me naked. As usual,
I decline. I bend, try catching embers
with bare fingers, crafting them as if to pluck
a petal. He points to the raven in the yard, mentions
the muffled feathers. I nod. Before his pistol
speaks into the swoop of my skull, the raven
tosses its head to clamor. This meant: *Come
quietly*. Lucky friend. When it covets, it caws.
My anatomy disagrees. Why make fuss. Pain
comes and goes. Inside the fire, a moth
dances. I desire its kiss. Like many animals,
I want it inside me. As his palm partitions
inhale and exhale, I picture what the raven
might be doing. I see it vaunt across
the lawn, stopping to dig its beak
into the dirt. The next time I breathe,
I'm face down. Transcendent, almost.
When he grabs my hand, I rest my lips
against. Silky moth wing. But it burns.
The fire barks, prays for our attention.
Greedy inferno. My throat leaps, joyous
for his finish.
     All this, says the raven, *and it never comes*.

Trayvon

Forced
      loose, bawling
as bullets
settle inside the hidden
      garden, budding
      once light slithers
from the moon to the eye—
lacquered
      with tears

and the after-speech:
      These assholes, they always
           get away.

His howls, I hear,
      storm, split, spit out
         before breath retreats
into the fleeing lung. Out of habit
      more howls pirouette
        the mouth,
      the mouth a night of its own
      where the teeth glisten
         already-faded stars—
still flared like a fire
of broken glass
        caught in sunlight.

I begin to flinch
as though seeing my fly-flooded figure
      reflected
through the gun's endless

iris.

    I bow my head, my eyes,
feel myself labor,
pull myself into the bathroom,

        the blind white,
        yank back
            the shower curtain.

Strip.
    Breathe.
        Get in.

Self-Portrait as Crow

I.

I've always been a sucker for being eaten alive.

One eye, like a dark rose, drips
from the fox's maw, spills its beauty.
Instead of "caw," it is *help* that adorns
my beak. As the petalled-eye hangs
there, watches me watch it unbloom
into the fox's taste,

an old wave of blackness washes over me.

I've never been more menaced.
Some of me stays when the fox leaves, flees
into the nearest greenery. I glitter a slow stain
to the buzz of the streetlight, its cross-
hatch smile across everything: *if only he'd stop
resisting, the poor bird would still be alive.*

II.

My gore lingers into the next dawn.
It is spring. The season brings me a wooden
casket to rest my remains. I'm wrapped
in traditional wear—earth tones and yellow.
Waiting. Flora broken beside me.

Before the sirens come, I summon a flock
of savages with my dead: a natural magic.

But this is nothing new. My brothers and sisters
raise their wings to the crowgods, I watch
the murder surround. Some sit at my limp, bow
heads of grief. Others remain a shadow hovering.
The silent ones cram pieces of anger
into the muscles' wax. Replace the protein.
Fuel their rage.

Boy

The pavement smell of black boys.
Write and wrap black boys. Bang blue against
those black boys. Black boys are sin.

Write them sin boys. Listen
to sin boys. Them sin boys whine like you
used to. They church like you used to.
Denied Jesus like you did. Front row pew boys.

Momma waits for you. Momma say Jesus will
save you black boy. Listen to that Jesus boy.
Write about them Jesus boys.
Nail yourself against that Jesus boy.

Stomach first.
Then nail.
Then palm.

Fracture the jaw. Unhinge the cheekbone.
Turn teeth into fire. Let the blood nest
on the lips: a puddle of bones.

Dead bones. Dead boned boy. Cause black
boys are left dead boy. Be balled up boys.
Be left boned and bone. And brown and brown
and
black boys.

Pavement smelling boys. Left wanting nothing
left of black boy.
Dead boy. Full of bones boy. Dead boned
boy. Wanting to be touched by men boy. Tear off
the skin cause it reeks of too touchy men
boy.

Remember how he felt you up with his palm boy?

Boy.

You need love boy. Cause boys like you are starting to look the same. Boys like you are beginning to look too much like tombstones than boys. Like chalk outlines than body. Bodied boy. Niggas in bodies boy. You nigga's boy. You every brown boy come before you boy.

Black boy burn bring black boy back breathe black boy breathe
boy burn black boy burn breathe bright blaze boy
     black
     black
     black brown boy bound boy bottom boys be bones be
bagged boy black boys bring bright boy being black boy no
bright boy be brown boy but brown boy burn boy
     'bolished boy black boy
break.

Alternate Ending with Weeping

But I am human. I repeat it. Finally. Without
him inside me. This open space where
once was skin. Was a pulled back shirt.
Was hands combing. Behind, there was
a backyard of things—I couldn't tell you
now. I'm sorry. I'm sure he was good. He said it,
sometimes when kissing. But without actually
saying. He would force a bend from me.
A degree to which meant, "welcome."
I didn't know, then. If anything, I was twinned
at the mouth. It was slender. Beside me,
an empty fireplace. That abyss. Growing
less happy. You have heard it before: *relax*. Relax? I instructed
nothing
of limbs: legs, arms, unballed fists.
I had to expand from the inside. Be brighter.
A window half-split to dawn's rituals: sunlight knitting the
basket of trees, winnows—
their melodies sitting on the sill, a man reading
on the front lawn across the street.

Riding with Death

He was the last stallion
     I rode,
dick-hungry: not yet
soot: my mouth
vanished
     behind the darkness—a pure
mammal, his bones unskinned
and I, spooled
     of rubies, opened like a zipper
stuck
     on its threads, seams clotted
     before stripped.
My face morphed
into one eye
     when the horse's hind
legs spoke
and I spoke and my thighs gripped
     the homely animal's ribcage,
each rib-bone
disappearing.
         But understand this: I loved him,
madly, meat seething romance,
clicked, dipped
     into the cold kiss of his thinness,
his wilderness
of maggots and waxwing moths gnawed
     the skull-sockets to static.
It was his naked that haunted—
     those skillet hips would swallow
my young suckling, jaw widened.
         Removed.

Still: if you look at him
now:
flat spine, trotting on four,
        maneless,
who'd think Grim Reaper? Satin cloak? Stainless
        scythe?

O poor Death, poor savage beast, you thought
my end would birth here, our bodies wrestling
                to become one nature.
You see, my love, I'm what the ancestors
engraved into the midnight indigo.
                        Infinite and godly:
when you arrived
        at my door, I whipped you
        on the ass
                and the ass bowed in my name
like a sunset.

Acknowledgments & Notes

"A Question of Rain" is after Jayson Smith.

"How We Forget" is after Loyce Gayo.

"Riding with Death" is written in response to Jean-Michel Basqiaut's painting, *Riding with Death*.

I am grateful to the following journals and magazines that first gave early versions of these poems a home:

About Place Journal—"How We Forget"
Columbia Poetry Review—"Any Black Thing"
Construction Literary Magazine—"Hominal"
Crabfat Magazine—"Alternate Ending with Weeping," "Clenched," and "Offering," part I; previously titled, "Keeper"
James Franco Review—"A Question of Rain"
Misrepresented People: Poetic Response to Trump's America—"Self-Portrait as Crow"
Muzzle Magazine—"Boy"
Solstice Literary Magazine—"Offering," part II
The Shallow Ends—"Trayvon"
Underblong—"Riding with Death"

My heart is full of gratitude to the following people for their wisdom, light, and encouragement. This book would not be what it is today without you:

Sarina Anderson, Jericho Brown, Franny Choi, Joshua Corson, jayy dodd, Aricka Foreman, Tariq Luthun, Jill Mceldowney, Raina McKinley, Sarah Maria Medina, Jonah Mixon-Webster, Jessica "Jade" Paul, Justin Phillip Reed, Donavin Whisler, L. Lamar Wilson, and Sung Yim.

To my Columbia College Chicago teachers—Lisa Fishman, Brian Mornar, Michael Robins, and Joshua Young—I thank you for pushing me.

Thank you Mary Jo Bang, francine j. harris, and Carl Phillips for continually guiding me while at Washington University in St. Louis.

For your guidance, patience, and tough love, CM Burroughs and Phillip B. Williams, I wouldn't be the poet I am today without you. Thank you.

Special thanks to Makia Chantel, Tyrone "Koach T" Crosby, Mayah Daniels, and Jermey Edmonson. I am standing today because of you. I cannot thank you enough.

Endless thanks to Bryan Borland and the Sibling Rivalry Press team for believing in this journey.

I am truly thankful for my family for loving me and caring for me in ways I may have not always seen. I love you.

About the Artist

Jalen Miller is a photographer interested in the phenomenon of matter and how presence alone impacts the observer. Through photography, Jalen seeks not to objectify, but to be a witness to *being*. For more, visit www.outlandishph.com.

About the Author

Luther Hughes is a Seattle native. He is the Founder/Editor-in-Chief of *the Shade Journal* and Associate Poetry Editor for *The Offing*. A *Windy City Times* Chicago: 30 Under 30 Honoree, his work has been published or is forthcoming in *Columbia Poetry Review, Vinyl, BOAAT, Tinderbox*, and others. Luther is currently an MFA candidate in the Writing Program at Washington University in St. Louis. You can follow him on Twitter @lutherxhughes. He thinks you are beautiful.

About the Press

Sibling Rivalry Press is an independent press based in Little Rock, Arkansas. It is a sponsored project of Fractured Atlas, a nonprofit arts service organization. Contributions to support the operations of Sibling Rivalry Press are tax-deductible to the extent permitted by law, and your donations will directly assist in the publication of work that disturbs and enraptures. To contribute to the publication of more books like this one, please visit our website and click *donate*.

Sibling Rivalry Press gratefully acknowledges the following donors, without whom this book would not be possible:

Liz Ahl

Stephanie Anderson

Priscilla Atkins

John Bateman

Sally Bellerose & Cynthia Suopis

Jen Benka

Dustin Brookshire

Sarah Browning

Russell Bunge

Michelle Castleberry

Don Cellini

Philip F. Clark

Risa Denenberg

Alex Gildzen

J. Andrew Goodman

Sara Gregory

Karen Hayes

Wayne B. Johnson & Marcos L. Martínez

Jessica Manack

Alicia Mountain

Rob Jacques

Nahal Suzanne Jamir

Bill La Civita

Mollie Lacy

Anthony Lioi

Catherine Lundoff

Adrian M.

Ed Madden

Open Mouth Reading Series

Red Hen Press

Steven Reigns

Paul Romero

Erik Schuckers

Alana Smoot

Stillhouse Press

KMA Sullivan

Billie Swift

Tony Taylor

Hugh Tipping

Eric Tran

Ursus Americanus Press

Julie Marie Wade

Ray Warman & Dan Kiser

Anonymous (14)

CPSIA information can be obtained
at www.ICGtesting.com
Printed in the USA
LVOW12s0915100118

562342LV00003B/69/P